RHETORIC AND POETIC IN THOMAS MORE'S *UTOPIA*

Humana Civilitas

Sources and Studies relating to
the Middle Ages and the Renaissance

Volume 5

Published under the auspices of

THE CENTER FOR MEDIEVAL AND RENAISSANCE STUDIES

University of California, Los Angeles

Rhetoric and Poetic

in

Thomas More's *Utopia*

Arthur F. Kinney

UNDENA PUBLICATIONS

Malibu, 1979

The emblem of
the Center for Medieval and Renaissance Studies
reproduces the imperial eagle of the gold *augustalis*
struck after 1231 by Emperor Frederick II;
Elvira and Vladimir Clain-Stefanelli,
The Beauty and Lore of Coins, Currency and Medals
(Croton-on-Hudson, 1974), fig. 130 and p. 106.

Library of Congress Card Number: 79-63658
ISBN: 0-89003-025-1 (hard cover only)

Undena Publications, P.O. Box 97, Malibu, Ca. 90265

Acknowledgments

I AM GRATEFUL to Fredi Chiappelli, Director, and Michael J. B. Allen, Assistant Director, of the Center for Medieval and Renaissance Studies at the University of California, Los Angeles, for first suggesting that I compose the present monograph; to Stephen J. Greenblatt, Harry Berger, A. R. Braunmuller, Elizabeth McCutcheon, and Richard A. Lanham, for their helpful criticisms of my first draft; to Professor John Carey and the Merton College, Oxford, Seminar and to the departments of English at the University of South Carolina, the University of New Mexico, the University of Georgia, the University of Toronto, Brown University, and the University of Massachusetts, Amherst, and to Nancy R. Lindheim, Emrys Jones, John Kerrigan, Barbara Kiefer Lewalski, and Donald Cheney, who in hearing later revisions provided further sharpening of my ideas. My appreciation also to Carol D. Lanham for editorial assistance in preparing copy for the press, and to Franz J. Strassmann for aid in proofing and checking source materials.

THE CHIEF DIFFICULTY in reading Thomas More's *Utopia* is knowing where we stand: are we to interpret the imaginary construct of Book II, Hythlodaeus's direct response to Book I, as a conjectural solution to European ills which were themselves real enough, or are we to realize that the land of Nowhere is, answerable construct or not, ironically imaginary? Raphael Hythlodaeus, in his flowing beard and robes, once gave the compass to the Utopians but he now stands self-alienated outside the courts and business chambers of Antwerp. Is he our potential pilot, then, or a prophet, or the court fool? Equally cogent cases could be made for each of these alternatives. Facing such bewildering possibilities, the writers who come recently before us falter.

The *Utopia*, H. G. Wells complained in 1935, is "one of the most profoundly inconsistent of books,"[1] while G. K. Chesterton remarks that "A mind like More's was full of light like a house made of windows; but the windows looked out on all sides and in all directions. We might say that, as the jewel has many facets, so the man had many faces; only none of them were masks."[2] So then the exasperation of Ruskin in a letter to F. S. Ellis some time before this, in July 1870. "What an infinitely

1. "Introduction" to *Utopia* (New York 1935), quoted in Ligeia Gallagher, ed., *More's "Utopia" and Its Critics* (Chicago 1964) p. v.
2. From a note in *The Universe*, an English weekly (1935), reprinted in *Moreana* 42 (1974) 66.

wise—infinitely foolish—book [*Utopia*] is!" he exclaimed. "Right in all it asks—insane, in venturing to ask it, all at once—so making its own wisdom folly for evermore; and becoming perhaps the most really mischievous book ever written."[3] So too Robbin S. Johnson, who sees (in the most recent detailed treatment of the *Utopia*) still new conundrums. "Hythlodaeus," Johnson writes, "is placed in the ironic literary situation of trying to transform fiction into reality, the negative into the positive, nothing into truth. In fact, since he has embodied this ideal in his own personality (which also does not exist, for he, like his ideal, is only a fiction), he pushes reality from both ends into the limbo of the fantastic."[4] Such a movement of mind and sensibility as Johnson proposes—from the desperate needs of men to the frustration or delusion of those wishing to service such needs—may be an apparent, rational way to approach a mischievous, paradoxical book like the *Utopia*. But it seems also to undermine More's seriousness of purpose during the two years and more he claims to have taken fashioning his treatise.

Utopia remains mischievous now as then because the problems it raises are so urgent, the treatment of them so transparently ironic. Raphael Hythlodaeus's eschatological revelations imply an etiology at once astonishingly forceful and dismayingly reductive; his arrogant, captious perspective quarrels with his professions of wisdom and humanity; even his name is disjunctive, for as the messenger of God/teller of trifles, he seems to cancel himself out. Can we give credence to this man who, the persona-More tells us, "was not so well acquainted with Latin as with Greek" (39)?[5] According to Harry Berger, Jr., this charac-

3. *The Works of John Ruskin*, ed. E. T. Cook and Alexander Wedderburn (39 vols. London 1903–12) 37.12.

4. *More's "Utopia": Ideal and Illusion* (New Haven 1969) 10.

5. Textual references to the *Utopia* are from the modified translation of G. C. Richards printed in vol. 4 of *The Complete Works of*

terization aligns Hythlodaeus with those Renaissance humanists who pride themselves on studying Greek speculation rather than Roman pragmatism, the visionaries rather than the governors, and this fits Hythlodaeus well enough.[6] But it may also be partly a joke: Hythlodaeus's superiority when condemning pride in others may suggest that he sees himself primarily as a philosopher aware of Greek, forgetting, in his less frequent employment of Latin, that to speak of imperfect human nature (even as reorganized in Utopia) is to speak only of trifling things. Thus Hythlodaeus's contribution in *Utopia* II becomes a tea-time declamation in a garden walled off from Antwerp, the capitalistic center of the world then known, his truly splendid attack on drones and thieves in *Utopia* I somehow (for Hythlodaeus) finding sufficient response in an epideictic oration on Utopia.

It is persona-More, so this line of reasoning runs, that is the responsible one; he is in Antwerp to do some negotiating, and he advocates in Book I the necessity for compromise and action. Yet this wise and learned persona-More describes himself in the same passage, and the deft, brief sketch amazes. "I am constantly engaged in legal business, either pleading or hearing, either giving an award as arbiter or deciding a case as judge. I pay a visit of courtesy to one man and go on business to another. I devote almost the whole day in public to other men's affairs and the remainder to my own. I leave to myself, that is to learning, nothing at all" (39). This active man is thus a *doer* of trifles, with no time or energy to understand God's messages. Between him and Raphael there is not much choice. Or is there?

This vexing problem of our relationship to the work

St. Thomas More, ed. Edward Surtz, S.J., and J. H. Hexter (New Haven 1965).

6. "The Renaissance Imagination: Second World and Green World," *The Centennial Review* 9 (1965) 63.

also vexed More's contemporaries and elicited from them a surprising range of responses. Budé sensed the play of wit in the *Utopia* but did not altogether deny its seriousness. His letter to Thomas Lupset contains its own, mirroring ironies.

I owe you really immense thanks, Lupset, most learned of young men, for having handed me Thomas More's *Utopia* and thereby drawn my attention to what is very pleasant reading as well as reading likely to be profitable. . . . I had the book by me in the country as I ran up and down very busily and gave directions to the workmen, for, as you have partly come to know by yourself and partly heard from others, I had been expending much energy on the business of my country estate now for the second year. As I learned and weighed the customs and laws of the Utopians, the reading of the book impressed me so much that I almost neglected and even forsook the management of household affairs. I perceived the trumpery in all the theory and practice of domestic economy and in absolutely all anxiety for increasing one's revenue.[7]

Others of More's peers are more singular in their orientation. But they do not help us much either, as C. S. Lewis discovered:

Erasmus speaks of [*Utopia*] as if it were primarily a comic book; Tyndale despises it as "poetry"; for Harpsfield it is a "iollye inuention," "pleasantly" set forth; More himself in later life classes it and the *Praise of Folly* together as books fitter to be burned than translated in an age prone to misconstruction.[8]

Lewis misrepresents the views of each of these men, and of More himself, because he draws general comments from specific contexts, but his point remains valid even so:

7. This letter first appeared in the 1518 edition of *Utopia*; the translation here is that in the Surtz–Hexter edition (n. 5 above) 5.

8. *English Literature in the Sixteenth Century Excluding Drama*, vol. 3 of *The Oxford History of English Literature* (Oxford 1954) 167.

More's contemporaries responded variously to the *Utopia* —at various times and variously from one another. They did not know where they stood either.[9] More seems not even to have known himself, torn as he was between admiration of the *Utopia* and apprehension of how it might be received, in his correspondence now pressing for publication, now dismissing it.

Among the Elizabethans, Sir Thomas Smith comments in his *De Republica Anglorum* of 1583 that Utopias are "feigned commonwealths, such as never was nor never shall be, vain imaginations, phantasies of philosophers, to occupy the time, and to exercise their wits."[10] A century later, in his second edition of 1684, the good bishop of Sarum, Gilbert Burnet, saw the *Utopia* as "intended to set many Notions in [the] Reader's way," causing him to work out his own response to Hythlodaeus's presentation of an ideal commonwealth.[11] "I cannot tell whether I should call him a foolishe wyseman, or a wyse foolishman," Edward Halle sums up in his chronicling of the Tudors, "for vndoubtedly he beside his learnyng, had a great witte, but it was so myngled with taunting and mocking, that it seemed to them that best know him, that he thought nothyng to be wel spoken except he had ministred some mocke in the communicacion."[12] Serious mockery and taunting gravity: Halle is thinking of Erasmus's *Moriae encomium* and the tradition of humanist rhetoric which invites precisely the kind of verbal *sprezzatura* that characterizes *Utopia* and confuses its readers. Halle's approach, historically grounded, is helpful even now. Seen

9. Some of these responses are conveniently gathered by Enid M. G. Routh in *Sir Thomas More and His Friends, 1477–1535* (London 1934; rpt. New York 1963) 77–78.

10. Quoted in Ernest E. Reynolds, *Saint Thomas More* (London 1953) 118.

11. *Utopia*, sig. A7v.

12. *The Vnion of the Two Noble and Illustre Famelies of Lancastre & Yorke* (1548 ed.) sig. PPP4v.

as originating in the joint translations of Lucian by Erasmus and More, the *Utopia* is, like the *Moriae encomium*, a witty because hyperbolic praise of the partly indefensible. Replace the *Utopia* in its original context and the strange medley of its tones—and its apparent cross-purposes—begins to be clarified.

Responde stulto iuxta stultitiam suam: "Answer a fool according to his folly" (Proverbs 26:5). Thomas More's fictional *Utopia* began as a deliberate reply to the fictional *Moriae encomium* of Erasmus. The two works are twinned, homologous: in a letter to Ulrich Hutten, Erasmus claims that More composed his response in much the same way, beginning with a wise and witty declamation, a monological praise of wisdom which later became Book II of the *Utopia* we now know, although it was first intended to be the entire work. Book II is thus analogous to the *Encomium*; it is a self-contained and self-referential speech in praise of the ideal commonwealth,[13] while Hythlodaeus, in delivering it, is in his combination of the reasonable and the unreasonable, the desirable and the mad, a reification of Erasmus's Folly.[14] About this More the author never leaves us in doubt. Hythlodaeus—"a man of advanced years, with sunburnt countenance and long beard and cloak hanging carelessly from his shoulder, while his appearance and dress seemed to me to be those

13. So André Prévost, *Thomas More, 1477–1535, et la crise de la pensée européenne* (Paris 1969) 84, and Richard J. Schoeck, "'A Nursery of Correct and Useful Institutions': On Reading More's *Utopia* as Dialogue," *Moreana* 22 (1969) 26. Erasmus's letter to Hutten (23 July 1519) is translated by Barbara Flower in Johan Huizinga, *Erasmus and the Age of Reformation* (Harper Torchbook ed. New York 1957) 231–39.

14. Direct linkages between the *Encomium* and the *Utopia* are frequent. Cf. the title-page of the 1515 Froben edition of the *Encomium* ("*non minus eruditis quam festivis*") with the title-page of the 1516 *Utopia* ("*nec minus salutaris quam festivus*"). Or cf. details within the

of a ship's captain," his character-More remarks (49)—a man both hermit/prophet and sea captain/voyager[15] and also humanist student who benefits from his knowledge of Plato and Aristotle and from his experiences on a Grand Tour, admires without reservation all he has seen and learned of Utopia, a country where "They are very fond of fools," *Moriones in delitijs habentur* (193). Hythlodaeus's stubborn orthopraxy, we find, is the ironic result of his misguided, self-righteous orthodoxy.

From the start, however, *Utopia* is rhetorically the more complex work of the two. While More selects some of Erasmus's targets—education and sport, logic and law, court life and church, even philosophy and religion—his spokesman Hythlodaeus not only praises but commends. *Utopia* II is more than an *encomium*; it is a demonstrative oration in full dress, which as Thomas Wilson, following Agricola, defines it in *The Arte of Rhetorique* (1553) "is a meane wherby we do praise, or dispraise thynges, as vertue, vice, tounes, citees, castles, woddes, waters, hilles, and moūtaines"; confirm them by proofs showing their honesty, profit, and execution; and then "teache men the truth of it." Only then "it were wel done & Oratourlike."

works; Folly, for example, is born on one of the "insulae fortunatae," or a land which figures Utopia itself. The title *Utopia* may come from Lucian, whose works More and Erasmus had studied and translated together. In *The Sale of Creeds* Lucian writes,

> Fifth Dealer: And now, what are the main features of your philosophy?
>
> Socrates: Ideas and types of things. All things that you see, the earth and all that is upon it, the sea, the sky—each has its counterpart in the invisible world.
>
> Fifth Dealer: And where are they?
>
> Socrates: Nowhere. Were they anywhere, they were not what they are.

Trans. H. W. and F. G. Fowler, *The Works of Lucian of Samosata* (4 vols. Oxford 1905) 1.198; see also A. R. Heiserman, "Satire in the *Utopia*," *PMLA* 78 (1963) 163–65.

15. Johnson (n. 4 above) 43–45.

Since a successful work of demonstrative rhetoric requires not merely praise but also truth, the advocate transforms himself into a sage, "the Logician shewes hymselfe." This is seen in the six places of logic that together account for Hythlodaeus's presentation of Utopia to Peter Giles, to John Clement, to the persona-More, and to us: also first found in Agricola's *De inventione dialectica libri tres* (written about 1479; printed 1515) and adopted by Wilson, these are definition, causes, parts, effects, things adjoining, and contraries. "I do not se otherwise," Wilson concludes, "but that these [places] of Logique must first be mynded ere thother can well be had."[16] While we may be surprised at how closely *Utopia* II conforms to Agricola's and Wilson's prescription of a traditional pattern of classical rhetoric, we may also note with what clarity Wilson's words distinguish it from the *Moriae encomium*. Erasmus's Folly asks only that we commend her to our delight; Hythlodaeus, as the author More's prolocutor, insists that everywhere we find him *reasonable*, sound in his ideas, logical in the sequence of his thoughts, and sensible in his applications of principles. In all this, Hythlodaeus is not merely the recorder or conveyer of Utopian thinking; he becomes a true *representative* of their society. When in our turn we become a piece of a logician, we are invited to judge the whole by his unsupported declamation.

Hythlodaeus testifies to Utopia as eudemonic, a country characterized by peace, stability, and democracy, which practices parliamentary government, a cooperative economy, and religious toleration and which advocates work and relaxation, family and social unity, and individual cultivation of learning and morality. This sempiternal land, moreover, has learned how to eliminate crime, poverty, war, and capital punishment and has therefore

16. *The Arte of Rhetorique* (1553) C4v–D1; facs. rpt. with intro. by Robert Hood Bowers (Gainesville Fla. 1962) 36–37.

released its citizenry from grief, from illness, and from despair. Such matters have real force for Hythlodaeus: his assiduity is heightened by the seriousness of his issues and the desirability of his ends—in this his stance is similar to More's and similar, surely, to our own—but he is also single-minded, innocent of Utopian weaknesses, and intolerant of questions and criticism; the thin veneer of his belief is vulnerable to the slightest assault.

As consequent, his is a speech of "passionate rhetoric," Richard S. Sylvester contends; "once started, his flow of words cannot be checked."[17] Like Folly, he begins slowly and traditionally, but soon emphases vary; testimony becomes tergiversation. He races over the governmental practices that seem more elective than they are, and lingers on the satisfactory distribution of goods; he speaks innocently of exploitation of slaves and unilateral restrictions on travel by the rulers of Utopia; and he emphasizes what passes, for Father Surtz and others, as epicureanism,[18] his concern at odds with his own criticism of epicurean practices. Hythlodaeus is, writes W. E. Campbell, "impatient, presumptuous, inexperienced and unbalanced in judgment,"[19] for like the Utopians whom he comes more and more to resemble in his speech of ironic dissembling, he refuses to modify his approbation of Utopia or translate it into useful counsel for societies beyond the Utopian boundaries such as that in which he meets the persona-More. Rhetoric here turns into rodomontade.

Elsewhere I have catalogued in some detail the

17. "'SI HYTHLODAEO CREDIMUS': Vision and Revision in Thomas More's *Utopia*," *Soundings* 51 (1968) 282. Sylvester thinks Hythlodaeus "begins to lose control of his tale," neatly enough, "in his mental journey concerning Utopian travel" (288).

18. Edward Surtz, S.J., *The Praise of Pleasure: Philosophy, Education, and Communism in More's "Utopia"* (Cambridge Mass. 1957) chaps. 4–7.

19. *More's Utopia and His Social Teaching* (London 1930) 48.

gross and subtle inconsistencies which awaken our interest and confirm our own thoughtful speculation;[20] alongside Erasmus's initial exercise they take their own clear shape. As with the *Moriae encomium*, which proceeds from harmless follies to serious immorality, Hythlodaeus's anfractuous picture of Utopia also grows singularly if unintentionally dark; and where Erasmus's Folly proceeds in the end to the wisdom of folly as a definition for Christianity, the *Utopia* ends, more hesitantly, on persona-More's unspoken reservations. This is in part because Hythlodaeus's narrowing perspective is not what we may anticipate from his denunciation of inhumanities in *Utopia* I: in *Utopia* II his views can be casuistic and *dys*topian. The regimented life of the common Utopian citizen repeatedly pulls him toward an identifiable community with unidentifiable persons in it; their common meals and look-alike clothing even make them analogous, within Hythlodaeus's own frame of mind, with the community of men punished for theft in *Utopia* I. "There can be no doubt that community of property, reinforced by the institutional discipline necessary to maintain it as an ideal, can eliminate manifestations of corruption," Robbin Johnson writes. "But the price is violence to the human being, a violence reflected vividly in Hythlodaeus' bellicose language and truculent 'defense.' And the error involved in seeing community of property as the ideal solution to the problems besetting man is that Hythlodaeus' communism, reinforced by institutional coercion, only eliminates the *manifestations* of corruption, not the *sources* of human wickedness."[21] Outside the tight little island, Utopians make war when they are attacked; they also remain ever ready to infiltrate peoples who they declare are their

20. "Rhetoric as Poetic: Humanist Fiction in the Renaissance," *ELH* 43 (1976) 413–43.
21. *More's "Utopia"* (n. 4 above) 140.

adversaries, hiring mercenaries and bribing others to arrest or kill their opponents.

So encouraging mercenary activity and thus reinforcing their own sense of superiority—"thinking that they would be the greatest benefactors to the human race if they could relieve the world of all the dregs of [the Zapoletans]" (209)—the Utopians display a fundamental inconsistency of attitude. Plainly enough, the Utopians are as dogmatic on the surface and as uncertain beneath as Hythlodaeus himself; the more we hear of them, the more acutely aware we become that their chief failure is the failure to trust each other. The spring which is made into a city reservoir for Amaurote, we are told, is fenced in lest someone poison the water; this community conduit, similar to those freely open to people of Tudor London at Cornhill and at West Cheaping Street, is in Utopia enclosed, guarded: a telling symbol of harbored fears. Indeed, nowhere do the Utopians display a desirable humanist faith in humanity. So plain is this, in fact, that the first English translator of More's Latin work seems to have made a point of it: Ralph Robinson changes the title for Book II from "of the Godly gouernement" in his first edition of 1551 (G5) to "of the politike gouernement" in the second edition of 1556 (G5v).

The writer More's achievement, then, is to use a traditional form of rhetoric—the demonstrative oration, as defined by Cicero and Quintilian and conveyed by schoolmasters like William Lily and textwriters like Agricola and Wilson—to reveal rhetorical sophistry. The very insistence and repetitiveness of Hythlodaeus's praise of wisdom seems foolish; beyond that, we have the clue supplied by his oxymoronic name. There is also the title of the work itself. In open imitation of the *Moriae encomium* which, punning, Erasmus meant to be read as *In Praise of Folly* or *In Praise of* [*Thomas*] *More*, the author More also awards his single book not one but two titles: *De Optimo Reipvblicae Statv Deqve noua insula Vtopia*. Sylvester tells us that these half-titles are antonymous,[22] as, at first glance, they surely are. But as applied to the two books of the *Utopia*, they are strikingly synonymous as well. The concept of "the best state of the commonwealth" renders a bitter indictment on the greed and rapacity that distinguishes the foreign and fiscal policies of Europe as described openly in Book I, but the new island of Utopia is no solution—as the use of war and trade in Utopia shows us, common ownership does not eliminate greed and rapacity in human nature, but only causes such actions to be more carefully channeled. Beneath the layers of proleptic rhetoric, only ostensibly epideictic, Utopia is potentially Europe rather than the other way round. It is interesting to note that a formal presentation designed to explain the ideal state instead cloaks the failings of the state and as a consequence, in the revelation of a myopic Hythlodaeus, only exposes them. As if in spite of itself, his rhetoric leads past fiction to truth.

We should not be surprised to find Thomas More using rhetoric first to define and then to dramatize and condemn Hythlodaeus, for he lived in the high age of humanist rhetoric when, Walter J. Ong tells us, rhetoric "included poetic" and literature "bore everywhere the mark of rhetorical flair and rhetorical control."[23] This extraordinary intellectual environment Thomas More seems to have much enjoyed, this heady juxtaposition of syntactic wit and firm direction; "He especially delighted in composing declamations," Erasmus writes Hutten, "and in these liked paradoxical themes, for the reason that this

22. "'SI HYTHLODAEO CREDIMUS'" (n. 17 above) 275.

23. *Rhetoric, Romance, and Technology* (Ithaca and London 1971) 6, 101.

offers keener practice to the wits."[24] In the *Utopia* Thomas More combines play of mind and word-play to insinuate satire and a measure of self-ignorance behind Hythlodaeus's febrile protestations on behalf of his ideal, communistic commonwealth.[25]

But the universal Tudor training in rhetoric did not always lead to truth, as Hythlodaeus's thrasonical oration shows; it could as easily lead *away* from truth, toward the making of fictions, as in the propagandistic orations of Thomas More's *Richard III.* We can easily locate the cause for this fiction-making in the classical *suasoriae*, the deliberative orations based on legend and history, first practiced in Greece and Rome, that came to be a staple of the Tudor grammar school. Such speeches are mentioned in Cicero's early work, the *De Inventione*, and particularly in the pseudo-Ciceronian *Rhetorica ad Herennium*; Suetonius tells us Cicero himself "declaim[ed] in Greek as well as Latin up to the time of his praetorship, and in Latin even when he was getting on in years."[26] Some generations later Seneca the Elder, called Seneca Rhetor, recorded a collection of model *suasoriae* of the type "X, in circumstances Y, deliberates"; fortunately, these Roman exemplars have partially survived.[27]

Although it is likelier that examples in Cicero and Quintilian, Caesar and Ovid, rather than these Senecan originals, provided models for young Tudor grammarians, Tudor schoolboys learned to prepare and deliver these brief, formal speeches that might praise, persuade, or counsel an imagined audience much as Hythlodaeus sets out to persuade the persona-More. We have some difficulty now in appreciating these grammar schools, as out-

24. Huizinga (n. 13 above) 238.

25. Cf. Ong (n. 23 above) 63.

26. *De grammaticis et rhetoribus*, 25.3, trans. J. C. Rolfe (Loeb ed., 2 vols.) 2.437.

27. Trans. Michael Winterbottom (Loeb ed., 2 vols.).

lined for us by T. W. Baldwin and Craig R. Thompson[28]—where the boys arose before dawn and spoke Latin, at work and play, throughout each and every weekday with a half-day on Saturday—but in such an environment these formal speeches apparently took their natural place. The boys might compose anything—true or fictional—so long as it was in agreement with the laws of necessity and probability; and they composed them often to a set of detailed circumstances which likewise used fiction to simulate reality. Later Renaissance examples, such as Antony's speech in Shakespeare's *Julius Caesar* and the various arguments of the devils in Milton's *Paradise Lost* II, holding strictly to the same form, show the residual force of such presentations in a rhetorically trained, rhetorically oriented culture.

Closely associated with these *suasoriae* was the figure of thought known as *prosopopoeia* in which the speaker imagines himself in a fictional role; it is, as Henry Peacham describes it in *The Garden of Eloquence* (1577), "the fayning of a person."[29] In the first of the seven *suasoriae* recorded by Seneca, Alexander debates whether to sail the ocean (as the Loeb edition titles it), and the speaker must pretend to be one of Alexander's war council *or* his mother, urging him not to sail, *or else to be* Alexander insisting that he will. In the second model *suasoria*, the speaker must imagine himself one of the Spartans at Thermopylae pressing his companions to stand and fight the Persians *or else* urging them to retreat; in the third, the speaker as Agamemnon tells Calchas why he refuses to sacrifice his daughter Iphigenia. An even larger number of themes for *suasoriae* are noted by Philostratus in his *Lives of the Sophists*.

28. Baldwin, *William Shakspere's Small Latine and Lesse Greeke* (2 vols. Urbana 1944); Thompson, *Schools in Tudor England* (Washington D.C. 1953; rpt. Charlottesville Va. 1973).

29. Facsimile rpt. Scolar Press (Menston England 1971) sig. Oiii.

Given such a prevalent model for writing, we can see the *Utopia* as a typical *suasoria*, in which Hythlodaeus imagines himself playing the part of a Utopian and counseling the young ambassador-lawyer More to commend their society; *or* we can view the *Utopia* as the author-More's witty practice of both sides at once: he will imagine a speech by Hythlodaeus in support of Utopia while attacking Europe, and *in the same work* he will also imagine a speech by the opposing viewpoint whom we call persona-More. That such verbal enactments are theatrical—that they lead to Erasmus's explicit and More's implicit notion that all the world is a stage and men merely foolish players on it—is also traceable to the satirist Lucian. In *Of Pantomime* 65, Lucian compares the art of rhetorical *prosopopoeia* with that of the pantomimic dancer.

The pantomime is above all things an actor: that is his first aim, in the pursuit of which he resembles an orator, and especially the composer of declamations, whose success, as the pantomime knows, depends like his own upon verisimilitude, upon the adaptation of language to character; prince or tyrannicide, pauper or farmer, each must be shown with the peculiarities that belong to him.[30]

Likewise in his doubling of voices, but especially in that of Hythlodaeus, Thomas More as the clever rhetorician beats Erasmus at his own game. And in doing so, he realizes Peacham's full (and traditional) definition:

Prosopeia [*sic*], the fayning of a person, that is, when to a thing sencelesse or dumme, wee fayne a fit persō, this figure Orators vse as well as Poets, an Oratoure by this Figure maketh the common welth to speake: lyfe and death: vertue and pleasure: honesty and profite: welth and pouerty: enuy and charity: to pleade and contend one agaynst another.[31]

30. Quoted by Donald Lemen Clark, *Rhetoric in Greco-Roman Education* (New York 1957) 222.

31. Peacham (n. 29 above) ibid.

Erasmus as Folly played the part of pleasure, profit, and charity, but More, as Hythlodaeus, "maketh the [very] common welth to speake."

"Rhetoric produced individuals predisposed to approach any subject by taking a side, because they were not formally trained to do anything else: any side, perhaps, but some side certainly," Ong writes with fine lucidity of the literary culture in which More found himself. "The life of the mind was exciting because it was framed in conflict."[32] We do not know if Thomas More had any formal training in *suasoriae* when staying with Cardinal Morton, although the practice of such imaginary declamations was so commonplace the tutor in the household might well have given him some themes to compose on; but surely, in the little academy More later established in his own home he would have had occasion to examine the formal training in Tudor grammar schools. What is certain, however, is that the judicial orations known as *controversiae*, growing out of the possible opposition of two differing deliberative orations practiced as *suasoriae*, as arguing for or against Alexander's voyage, were the primary method of education in the Henrician Inns of Court when More studied there. We know they attracted More's wit, too, because he and Erasmus vied in writing their own *controversiae* in response to a standard one on tyrannicide when they were translating Lucian.[33]

32. "Tudor Writings on Rhetoric, Poetic, and Literary Theory," chap. 3 of *Rhetoric, Romance, and Technology* (n. 23 above) 65, 66.

33. Erasmus had great praise for declamations. "I greatly desire that this sort of exercise—no other is more fruitful—should be restored to our schools. For if we were diligently drilled from boyhood in this exercise of declamation, following the precepts of Cicero and Quintilian and the ancient examples, there would not be, in my opinion, such a dearth of good speaking among those who profess oratory publicly" (*Opera*, 1703 ed., I.265; quoted in Clark [n. 30 above] 260).

Classical *controversiae* as the Tudors understood them are the distant ancestors of our present-day college debates; and, at the risk of parody, we might transcribe the *Utopia* into one of them: "Resolved, That the common ownership of goods and services is the basis for an ideal society." The *controversiae*, fixed paradoxes presented by contradictory (but actual) Roman laws, are recorded by Seneca the Elder, along with epigrams and amusing anecdotes; they appear too in Livy. They invite the young lawyer to defend the wife who slew her tyrant husband, or the man who repudiated an agreement to allow the foster father of his children to retain them when he has a change of heart, or the brave veteran, maimed and without hands, accused of murder.

One of the earliest *controversiae* recorded in Roman rhetoric appears in Cicero's *De Inventione*:

> Law: A tyrannicide shall receive the reward commonly given to victors at the Olympic games and he shall ask the magistrate for whatever he wishes, and the magistrate shall give it to him. Another law: When a tyrant has been slain the magistrate shall execute his five nearest blood-relations. Alexander, who had set himself up as tyrant at Pherae in Thessaly, was killed by his wife, named Thebe, at night, when he was in bed with her. She demands as a reward her son whom she had by the tyrant. Some say that the boy ought to be executed according to law. The case is brought before a court.

Cicero's accompanying advice relies solely on adeptness at law. Where the same topics of invention may favor either side, he instructs the readers of *De Inventione*, the lawyer must consider "the most important matters, that is the most expedient, honourable or necessary"; "in the second place, [the lawyer] should consider which law was passed last, for the latest law is always the most important; then which law enjoins some action and which permits, for that which is commanded is necessary, that which is permitted is optional; then in which law a penalty is prescribed for non-compliance or which law has the greater penalty, for that law has the highest claim to be upheld in which the penalties are most carefully prescribed," and so on.[34]

Such an exercise would be argued at the Inns of Court, with those who took the wife's part and those who opposed her choosing whatever topics of invention an act of *prosopopoeia* might indicate. "So long as a theme did indeed force the student to think through an intricate lawyer's puzzle," Donald Lemen Clark writes in *Rhetoric in Greco-Roman Education*, "the teachers seemed not to care even if the theme involved the acceptance of impossibilities, perversions of history, and non-existent laws."[35] And Clark might well have added, if he had had the Tudor world as well as the classical world in mind, "and the teachers seemed not to care if the theme involved the acceptance of imaginary lands, perversions of human nature, and non-existent customs."

Another famous *controversia* which Clark relates is given the traditional title of "The Poor Man's Bees." It is the thirteenth of the major declamations traditionally attributed to Quintilian. Clark sums it up this way:

"The law allows an action for injuries suffered wrongly (*injuria*). A poor man and a rich man were neighbors in the country; their gardens joined. The rich man had flowers in his garden; the poor man, bees. The rich man complained that his flowers were injured by the poor man's bees. He demanded that the bees be removed. When the poor man failed to remove them, the rich man sprinkled poison on his flowers. The poor man's bees all died of the poison. He brings action against the rich man for injuries suffered wrongfully." (247)

34. *De Inventione* II.xlix.144–46, trans. H. M. Hubbell (Loeb ed.) 313–15.

35. Clark (n. 30 above) 230.

Whatever *controversiae* Thomas More apprenticed to before writing *Utopia*, we know from Stapleton's biography of him that Margaret Roper practiced on "The Poor Man's Bees." "In imitation or rather emulation of Quintilian," Stapleton notes, "she defended the rich man"; and of her choice he observes, "Because to defend him is the more difficult, Margaret's art and eloquence should be seen to be the more excellent."[36] She took the task of defense as a challenge. But the choice was hers, as it was that of the Tudors' masters Cicero and Quintilian before her. Cicero stressed in the *De Oratore* that the development of powerful speeches cannot—as the early Greek rhetoricians wished—always be scientifically reducible to rules. Such speeches are instead the product of creative imagination and eloquent art, of fanciful embroidery of facts and simulation of situations, to make the most of existing materials and opportunities. Cicero especially, George Kennedy tells us, became "almost equally adept at argument, at presentation and destruction of character, and emotional appeal."[37] We need not look further for Hythlodaeus's model in *Utopia* II when he seizes the chance to tell of a wondrous land and exhausts the afternoon—and so precludes a response from persona-More—in his energetic defense of Nowhere.

This sort of activity was characteristic of much of Thomas More's life at the time he composed *Utopia*. "Let us never forget," Richard J. Schoeck cautions us, "that he was continuously a busy man of the law, who spent most of his waking hours in by far the greatest portion of his adult life reading petitions and other legal documents,

36. Thomas Stapleton, *D. Thomae Mori Angliae quondam cancellarii vita*, in *Tres Thomae* (Douai 1588) chap. 11; quoted by Clark (n. 30 above) 250.

37. These remarks are a paraphrase of George Kennedy, *The Art of Rhetoric in the Roman World, 300 B.C.-A.D. 300* (Princeton 1972) 225–26; the quotation is from page 275.

hearing evidence and questioning witnesses, giving legal opinions or decisions."[38] To this judgment we may join Erasmus's first-hand observation: "Although the young man's mind born for better things not unreasonably revolted from [the law], nevertheless, after sampling the scholastic disciplines he worked at the law with such success that none was more gladly consulted by litigants, and he made a better living at it than any of those who did nothing else, so quick and powerful was his intellect."[39] And so engaged, he learned, from his study of the *suasoriae* and *controversiae* onward, to *create* the best cases, exactly as William Roper will show Richard Rich and Thomas Cromwell creating their own best cases against More to bring about his execution for high treason.

The profession of English jurisprudence, Erasmus wrote Hutten in connection with his portrait of More, "is quite unconnected with true learning." Rather, as Cicero and Quintilian knew and as Hythlodaeus realizes (if he does not recognize it) in his *encomium*, in Tudor England as in classical Rome, "The trial was like a great drama in which the people crowding on the steps of the tribunal made Cicero think of the audience in the theatre to see a show. The very language of the law court [had] gone over into the theatre. The cases were divided into sections known as *actiones* and the prosecutor was known as an *actor*."[40] No wonder playwrights like John Heywood and John Rastell felt so at home in the More circle. As for his defense of Utopia, Hythlodaeus comes, once he is past his initial, "factual" description, to realize that both he and Nowhere itself are on trial, and it is thus—as defendant and defender—that he takes his part along with persona-More, in More's

38. "Common Law and Canon Law in Their Relation to Thomas More," in *St. Thomas More: Action and Contemplation*, ed. Richard S. Sylvester (New Haven and London 1972) 21–22.

39. In the letter to Hutten quoted by Huizinga (n. 13 above) 235.

40. Kennedy (n. 37 above) 18.

reply to the *Moriae encomium*, on the author More's great stage of fools.

This persistent reliance on humanist rhetoric for the form and function of *Utopia* constitutes More's finest tribute to Erasmus. For as the premier educator and progenitor of English humanism, Erasmus advocated rhetoric as medular to the New Learning: in his clear, flexible Latin, Erasmus's first venture as teacher to an unknown readership was to make an epitome of Valla's *Elegantiae*, a study of rhetoric, eloquence, and persuasion; his own subsequent *De Ratione Studii, the Right Method of Instruction*, composed at the request of John Colet in 1511, urged Tudor grammar schools to emphasize "exercises in formal Oratory—a declamation in praise of Socrates, or in denunciation of Caesar; . . . for the married life or against it; against pilgrimages or in praise of them."[41] Adhering to classical antecedents, Erasmus and his followers make no distinction between learning rules and composing fictions, between process and product. The art of learning is learning an art. John Rainoldes echoes an Erasmian culture when he praises their common master Cicero as "eloquentium prudentissimus, prudentium eloquentissimus,"[42] the wisest of the eloquent and the most eloquent of the wise: Quintilian's rational premise that the good orator must first be a good man is strikingly corrupted to mean that eloquence (and eloquence alone) *becomes*, because it translates, wisdom. This questionable premise also lies behind Hythlodaeus's exultant epideictic oration in *Utopia* II.

It is precisely this assumption, crescive but already

41. Trans. William Harrison Woodward, *Desiderius Erasmus concerning the Aim and Method of Education* (Cambridge 1904; rpt. New York 1964) 172.

42. *Oratio in Laudem Artis Poeticae* [*circa 1572*], ed. and trans. William Ringler and Walter Allen, Jr. (Princeton 1940) 42.

influential, which shapes Erasmus's best-known textbook for St. Paul's School, London, the *De Copia.* Here Erasmus urges eloquence through varying words, simplifying thoughts, and supplying pictorial detail that aligns oratory with poetry. "If someone should say that a city was captured," he writes, paraphrasing Quintilian (VIII.3.67),

> he doubtless comprehends in that general statement everything that attends such fortune, but if you develop what is implicit in the one word [i.e. captured], flames will appear pouring through homes and temples; the crash of falling buildings will be heard, and one indefinable sound of diverse outcries; some will be seen in bewildered flight, others clinging in the last embrace of their relatives; there will be the wailing of infants and women, old people cruelly preserved by fate till that day, the pillaging of profane and sacred objects, the running about of those carrying off booty and those seeking it, prisoners in chains before their captors, and the mother struggling to keep her infant, and fighting among the victors wherever there is greater plunder.[43]

Such directions, which renew the application of imagining (of *making* as *making up*) to a rhetorical situation, were endlessly popular: the *De Copia*, published first by Badius in Paris in 1512, went through 180 editions in the sixteenth century, 144 of them before 1572. Here, then, in the employment of *copia* to realize situation, analogous to the technique of *prosopopoeia* in recognizing *persona*, we find the basis for Hythlodaeus's careful description of the orderly, compartmentalized geography of Utopia, his account of the Utopians' childhood training and their adult leisure, and his luxuriant detail concerning their religion of pleasure. His foolishness lies not only in the substance of his praise but also in his misapplication and misdirection of

43. *De Utraque Verborum ac Rerum Copia* [*On Copia of Words and Ideas*], trans. Donald B. King and H. David Rix (Milwaukee 1963) 47–48.

standard Erasmian technique; the joke is that, failing to persuade persona-More or us, Hythlodaeus's rhetorical strategies nevertheless persuade *him*.

In writing *Utopia* to honor Erasmus (as well as to respond to him), Thomas More assumes that Erasmus and the other humanist readers of *Utopia* recognize rhetoric as the means to debate any side of any issue. Thus his indications throughout the work that Hythlodaeus is cold, inflexible, and dogmatic make their own pronouncement, the more so since persona-More urges compromise and adaptability on Hythlodaeus only to be coldly rebuked. Hythlodaeus practices, in both parts of *Utopia*, an art form he does not understand. That is why, by the end of *Utopia* II, we find his position in his unfinished debate with persona-More so exposed and self-condemning. In an age raised on *suasoriae* and *controversiae*, so single-minded an *encomium* on Hythlodaeus's part would be charged inherently with its own counterstatements; that he fails to comprehend this and so defend himself against them—substituting declamation for response to an implicit disputation—shows the rhetorical limitation of his position and the subtle, learned wit of Thomas More. These assumed conventions of rhetoric likewise answer our initial inquiry: they respond to the chief difficulty in reading *Utopia* by telling us where to stand. They tell us too what Harpsfield means when he calls *Utopia* a "iollye inuention."

But Harpsfield's description of the *Utopia* has not won universal acceptance because Thomas More's work strikes us not only as rhetorically witty but also as serious and committed. We know from Erasmus's letter to Hutten, furthermore, that More withheld circulation of *Utopia* II until, more than a year later, he had completed *Utopia* I, in which his scorn over capital punishment for thieves and his anger at the dispossessed ruined by enclosures carry a sharpness undenied by his wit and unreconciled by the bland and even, at times, pompous picture of the ideal community in *Utopia* II. The author More's concern seems to us now to be real enough; but how, in a rhetorical culture where presumed truths may be nothing more than clever fictions, where the "circumstances" in a *suasoria* may be "imagined" consequences of the figure *prosopopoeia*, can a justified concern be expressed seriously? How can one guarantee the return trip, bringing fiction back to truth? How can the author More, assured we will see the debate between persona-More and Hythlodaeus as the rhetorical exercise in irony that it is, still remain confident we will also acknowledge his passionately troubled statements on injustice and poverty? The lawyer's humane pleas for deserving defendants could be seen too easily as just another act of eristics.

The rhetorical author More who conceives of *Utopia* II as a *suasoria* and the whole of *Utopia* as a *controversia* must have been painfully aware each day that ingenious and extravagant verbal strategies among his fellow Tudors trained at grammar schools, universities, and Inns of Court could lead too frequently to acts of sophistry in which the worse is made to appear the better part, *hoc est hominem esse; anything*, in fact, could be made to seem wise, true, or necessary. As a consequence, those who bemoaned the loss of valid language in Thomas More's England came to share the skepticism they discovered in Sextus Empiricus. "Rhetoric," Sextus professes,

> declares this to be its main task,—how, for instance, we are to make small things great and great things small, or how just things may be made to appear unjust, and the unjust just. And in general, as rhetoric consists of opposite statements, one cannot say that the refined speaker is an orator, but the unrefined no longer an orator. For the orator, of whatever sort he may be, must certainly practise himself in contradictory speeches,

and injustice is inherent in contradictions; therefore every orator, being an advocate of injustice, is unjust.[44]

Sextus's charges against rhetoric begin by citing Plato's comment that rhetoric, having efficacy in words themselves, is persuasive but not instructive.[45] Sextus alludes to the *Gorgias* where Plato links sophists with the base trades of cookery, face-painting, fawning, and bewitching, since they deal with neither art nor poetry; Plato's attack lays the ground for his comparison of the poet to the lunatic (or one without true reason) in the *Ion* and his decision to banish all poets from his ideal *Republic*.

But it is Plato who also manages to reserve other grounds for establishing a usable poetic, and he does so at precisely the point we have now reached—he discusses good art as the avoidance of sophistry. This statement of Plato's comes where we might least expect to find it, but in a work that the lawyer More might have known: the middle or late dialogue *The Sophist*. Here an Elean Stranger informs Theaetetus (in the presence of Theodorus and Socrates) of two fundamental kinds of art—icastic and fantastic. Both kinds of art are what the Stranger calls *productive* rather than *acquisitive* (219A–C), for they are not acquired from things already existing but bring into being something new. These two kinds of art are, according to Plato, different in process and so identifiably distinct in their final products. Icastic or "likeness-making art" occurs "whenever anyone produces the imitation by following the proportions of the original in length, breadth, and depth, and giving, besides, the appropriate colours to each part" (235D–E)—when the artist records simply, without an intervenient imagination. Fantastic

44. *Against the Professors*, II.46–47, trans. R. G. Bury (Loeb ed., 4 vols.) 4.211.

45. *Gorgias* 453A; the passage comparing sophistry with base trades is *Gorgias* 463A–C.

art, on the other hand, either creates that which does not exist or gives a disproportionate, faulty representation of the object being imitated—it "produces appearance," Plato says, "but not likeness" (236C). Icastic art copies the original exactly. Fantastic art is exemplified by

> those who produce some large work of sculpture or painting. For if they reproduced the true proportions of beautiful forms, the upper parts, you know, would seem smaller and the lower parts larger than they ought, because we see the former from a distance, the latter from near at hand. . . . So the artists abandon the truth and give their figures not the actual proportions but those which seem to be beautiful, . . . but which would not even be likely to resemble that which it claims to be like, if a person were able to see such large works adequately (235E–236B).[46]

Representation, re-presentation, is the end of both forms of art, but the means are radically opposed. Icastic art conveys by reproducing an object; fantastic art necessarily distorts its subject. Both *recreate*, *make* by *making up*, but fantastic art recreates the appearance only, not the substance; it succeeds because it allows for a subjective, or displaced, perspective. It *persuades* the viewer to accept the fantastic art form as icastic, to accept what *seems* to be for what *is*. Plato's terms, already a nascent poetics because of his examples from painting and sculpture, are meant to divide truth from sophistry in his own sophistically rhetorical age.

When we turn to the *Utopia*, written in a second rhetorical age wary of sophistry, we see how this distinction between icastic and fantastic art can guide us in understanding the functioning of Thomas More's ironic work of humanist wit, as we have seen how an understanding of *suasoriae* and *controversiae* helps us to re-cog-

46. *The Sophist*, trans. Harold N. Fowler (vol. 2, Loeb ed. of Plato) 333–35.

nize and so recognize its form. Generally speaking, *Utopia* I is icastic; *Utopia* II, fantastic. Ignoring for the moment the *prosopopoeiae* of persona-More and Hythlodaeus, we find that the concrete objects represented by the imagination in *Utopia* I have, for More's readers, a clear, ordered, and reasoned correspondence to fact, while the concrete objects in *Utopia* II are often simulated and unreal. Given the context of art in his time, the author More opens the *Utopia* with a likeness of an actual event: his commission to Flanders in the company of Cuthbert Tunstal, Master of the Rolls. There is the trip to Antwerp and the visit with Peter Giles, clerk of Antwerp's court of justice, and references to the unfinished church of Notre Dame in Antwerp and to John Cardinal Morton in England.

The main grounds of argument also represent fact. We learn in *Utopia* I that in Cardinal Morton's England thieves "were everywhere executed, . . . as many as twenty at a time being hanged on one gallows" (61), while certain lines in John Skelton's "Speake Parrot" of 1521—"So many thevys hangyd, and thevys never the lesse"—and Harrison's comment in the essay appended to the 1587 edition of Holinshed's *Chronicles*—that "It appeareth by Cardane . . . how Henrie the eight, executing his laws verie seuerlie against such idle persons, I meane great theeues, pettie theeues and roges, did hang vp threescore and twelue thousand of them in his time"[47]—show how prevalent capital punishment for thieves really was. The commensurability of this punishment was a frequent point of debate in Thomas More's day; in his later "Debellation," the author More writes, "The iudges parte is to see that the punishemente passe not the grauitie of the offence" (*Works* [1553], sig. P6v).

Inequality of fortune among the English is another chief issue in *Utopia* I: alongside the poor and wretched

47. *Utopia* (n. 5 above) 315.

yearning to have more, others displayed, ostentatiously, sumptuous clothes (69). The plight of the poor is a common subject of the time in the poetry of Alexander Barclay and Skelton and in the famous dialogue between Thomas Lupset and Reginald Pole by Thomas Starkey, while Thomas More himself composed an epigram "To Euparíphus, Who Mortgaged His Farm to Buy Clothing."[48]

The matter of enclosures is more complicated. Surely historians now agree that the soil in Tudor England was still good enough for widespread farming, and recent work by Joan Thirsk and David M. Bevington[49] indicates that enclosures were confined largely to the Midlands and even there were decreasing as a problem by the time of *Utopia.* Yet in 1516 there was an act against "Pulling down of Towns" (7 Henry VIII), and in 1517 and subsequently, Commissions of Inquiry Touching Inclosures were formed all over Tudor England.[50] Such commissions were to investigate precisely those evils cited in *Utopia* I: engrossing (charging high interest), forestalling (buying up in advance so as to inflate the market price), and the pulling down of farms and villages for increased pasturage. The splendid Surtz-Hexter edition of *Utopia* is thick with annotations citing contemporary documents, statutes, and commentaries for the concrete images of *Utopia* I.

Such icastic art recedes in *Utopia* II, however, which focuses on the unreal, or fantastic, practices of Nowhere: the common meals and look-alike houses, the regimented dress and travel, the early-morning lessons

48. *The Latin Epigrams of Thomas More*, ed. Leicester Bradner and Charles Arthur Lynch (Chicago 1953) 211.

49. Thirsk, *Tudor Enclosures* (London 1959); also "Industries in the Countryside," in *Essays in the Economic and Social History of Tudor and Stuart England*, ed. F[rederick] J[ack] Fisher (Cambridge (1961) 70–88; Bevington, "The Dialogue in *Utopia*: Two Sides to the Question," *Studies in Philology* 58 (1961) 503, reprinted as "The Divided Mind" in *Twentieth Century Interpretations of "Utopia,"* ed. William Nelson (Englewood Cliffs N.J. 1968) 82–83.

50. Cited by Leslie Paul, *Sir Thomas More* (London 1953) 97.

and apprenticeships on farms, the naked betrothals and golden chamberpots. Hythlodaeus's ideal land is, we see at once, a faulty re-presentation of society because it is plotted on a distorted conception of human nature. The humanist trust so strikingly absent from the enforced community of *Utopia* II is the direct result of Hythlodaeus's proportionate distrust in humanity. Plato's discussion of proper art in *The Sophist* thus points directly to what is wrong in *Utopia* II; it also locates the cause. Hythlodaeus's art is faulty because his perspective is skewed: he sees Utopia from within, *as a Utopian.* He is, in Plato's terms, too close to his representation to be anything but subjective: Giles notes, when he jokingly writes to Busleiden, that as a Utopian Hythlodaeus finally returned to Utopia. It is, rather, the persona-More—and better yet ourselves—who command distance and objectivity, who see the whole piece of oratory as sophistic, persuading us by appearances and form rather than by substance and authenticity. Worse, Hythlodaeus's Utopia is not only disproportionate; it is irrational—a deformation of humanist reason. In Utopia men who hire mercenaries nevertheless stockpile their own military strategies; there citizens are encouraged to read while the country maintains a limited library. They desire peace yet have no hesitation over annexing territory not their own, claim selflessness yet remain imperialistic.

These extremes, between a real England portrayed in a real Antwerp in *Utopia* I and an irrational Nowhere in *Utopia* II, retain a general opposition—two halves of a rhetorical *controversia*, the juxtaposition of icastic and fantastic art. But the distinctions are not always sharp and absolute. For it is the fantastic Hythlodaeus who supplies much of the factually grounded criticism in *Utopia* I, while Nowhere in *Utopia* II resembles, in its pseudo-history, geography, and bicameral government, Thomas More's own England rather than a strange and unknown land. Surely this is part of Thomas More's wit. That we are to join, then, as well as oppose the two parts of *Utopia* is clear—not only in the fact that both are incorporated in the same time and setting, make use of the same characters, and are introduced by the same prefatory letter to Peter Giles, but also in the detailed description of Nowhere and Amaurotum which, opening *Utopia* II as if talking of England and London, recalls *Utopia* I and so solidly binds the work. The two halves of *Utopia* are identical in another way: in both, Hythlodaeus begins factually; then, falling in love with his own rhetorical and poetic powers, exaggerates (on the matter of English enclosures, for example; or concerning Utopian liberty) and finally is victimized by his pride which leads to his proposing the irrational and the outrageous (the end of capital punishment for thievery in a country of scarcity and the substitution of regimented separation from the human community in *Utopia* I; the elimination of private ownership and private identity in *Utopia* II).

Again and again, in each independent scene and in the *Utopia* as a whole, the author More moves from icastic to fantastic art, from the reasonable to the deformation of reason. He moves from the possible through the improbable to the impossible. Yet the whole movement is contained within a single rhetoric and poetic—and contained too within the fictional proposition with which it begins. Hythlodaeus's own deformation is caused by the pride he condemns in *Utopia* I and personifies throughout *Utopia* I and II—personifies to such an extent that the gentle, rational persona-More feels unable to argue a single issue with him at the close. By such subtle indicators, born of a rhetorical necessity and a Platonic poetics known in his time, Thomas More is able to criticize his England in a complex work of humanist art that is an appropriate response—and more—to Erasmus's *Moriae encomium*.

But the *Utopia* does more than rescue rhetorical technique for a humanist, educative art in an age of eristics; it also transcends its time in the poetics More formulates, just as Plato's discussion of icastic and fantastic art, exceedingly slight in *The Sophist*, becomes a central issue in several important treatises on imagination and poetry from the time of the *Utopia* onward.[51] In Italy, for instance, Patrizi, in *La deca disputata*, prefers the figure of icastic art (which he calls *effigy*) to the *image* of fantastic art because effigies particularize ideas. In the *Poetica*, Castelvetro tests all inventions by their icastic properties, dismissing fantastic art because it is not verisimilar. One of the few exceptions to the general preference for icastic art is taken in the *Della difesa della Commedia di Dante* III, where Mazzoni finds icastic art too close to history, and elects something more akin to fantastic art which he describes as "marvelous-credible." Debate in Italy on icastic and fantastic art came finally to rest on the widespread distinction made between Tasso's *Gerusalemme liberata*—his 1585 *Apologia in difesa della sua Gerusalemme agli Accademici della Crusca* claims he was influenced by Plato's definitions in *The Sophist* when he began his epic—and the opposing alternative, Ariosto's *Orlando Furioso*, generally considered the epitome of fantastic art.[52]

English apologists for poetry in the later days of this second high age of rhetoric also continue to argue for icastic art because of its lifelike properties. In his dedication to *The Revenge of Bussy D'Ambois*, George Chapman

51. There are important surveys of these works in Baxter Hathaway, *The Age of Criticism: The Late Renaissance in Italy* (Ithaca 1962) and Bernard Weinberg, *A History of Literary Criticism in the Italian Renaissance* (2 vols. Chicago 1961); a useful anthology of excerpts is in Erwin Panofsky, *Idea* (Berlin 1924) 96–98 n. 144 (= English trans. by Joseph J. S. Peake [Columbia S.C. 1968] 215 n. 51). I am also indebted to conversations with Katherine Duncan-Jones and D. H. Craig.

52. Hathaway (n. 51 above) 13–16, 350–51, and 390–91; Weinberg (n. 51 above) 2.636–46.

argues that the poet creates "things like truth," while Ben Jonson, in *Discoveries*, agrees that a "fainer" is one who "writes things like the Truth."[53] A fantastic poetics, on the other hand, results in unreal, freakish images. "This imagination," comments Juan Huarte Navarro in his *Examen de Ingenios* Englished by R. C. in 1594, "hath force not onely to compound a figure possible with another, but doth ioyne also (after the order of nature) those which are vnpossible, and of them growes to shape mountains of gold, and calues that flie." Such a commonplace attitude lies behind the complaint of John Davies of Hereford that "*Fantacie* / . . . doth so forme, reforme, [that] it deformes," and behind Spenser's figure of Phantastes with his chamber filled with "leasings, tales, and lies."[54]

But the English, like the Italians, also developed the Platonic dichotomy in their own ways. For Puttenham, proportion and disproportion become infused with humanist reason; he distinguishes in *The Arte of English Poesie* between ordered and disordered art, or what he calls the eufantastic and the fantastic. "Wherefore such persons as be illuminated with the brightest irradiations of knowledge and of the veritie and due proportion of things," he writes, "they are called by the learned men not *phantastici* but *euphantasiote* and of this sorte of phantasie are all good Poets, notable Captaines stratagematique, all cunning artificers and enginers, all Legislators Polititiens and Counsellours of estate, in whose exercises the inuentiue part is most employed and is to the sound and true iudgement of man most needful."[55]

53. Chapman: ed. Robert J. Lordi, Jacobean Drama Studies 75 (Salzburg 1977) "The Epistle Dedicatory," p. 41 line 24; Jonson: vol. 8, *Poems, Prose Works*, ed. C. H. Herford and Percy and Evelyn Simpson (Oxford 1947) 635.

54. Huarte Navarro: *The Examination of Mens Wits . . .* (London 1594; facs. rpt. Amsterdam and New York 1969) 132; Davies: *Mirum in Modum* (London 1602) sig. B3; Spenser: *Faerie Queene*, II.ix.51.

55. [George Puttenham], *The Arte of English Poesie* (London 1589; facs. rpt. Menston England 1968) sig. Diiii.

As for Sidney, his Puritan leanings cause yet another metamorphosis inspired by an openly pragmatic, explicitly Christian humanism while using nearly the same illustration we found first in Plato.

For I will not denie, but that mans wit may make *Poesie*, which should be [*eikastike*] which some learned haue defined figuring foorth good things to be [*phantastike*] which doth contrariwise infect the fancie with vnwoorthie obiects, as the Painter should giue to the eye either some excellent perspectiue, or some fine Picture fit for building or fortification, or containing in it some notable example, as *Abraham* sacrificing his sonne *Isaack*, *Iudith* killing *Holofernes*, *Dauid* fighting with *Golias*, may leaue those, and please an ill pleased eye with wanton shewes of better hiddē matters.[56]

Sidney links the infected will with fantastic art and the erected wit with icastic art because it is icastic art, truly representing God's creation or the poet's analogous creative act, which moves men to virtue.

Such various developments of the terms *icastic* and *fantastic* in the hands of Patrizi, Castelvetro, and Mazzoni, Navarro, Puttenham, and Sidney reveal the potency and utility of Plato's original distinction, and display the rich multitude of possibilities inherent in his initial descriptions. These variations on a theme follow the *Utopia*, some of them by more than a half-century, yet looking backward we see that they, too, insure a renewed validity for the *Utopia* in the revitalized humanism under Elizabeth I; they may well have taught later Tudors how to read the most significant humanist work by their most important Tudor predecessor. The reverse is also true: the achievement of the *Utopia* can be measured not only by the Erasmian rhetoric and Platonic poetic known in More's time but through the ageless, infinite variety by which it might come most to satisfy. Puttenham and Sidney, know-

56. Sir Philip Sidney, *The Defence of Poesie* (1595; facs. rpt. Menston England 1968) sig. G2.

ing where they stand on matters of humanist rhetoric and poetic, suggest to us further a Hythlodaeus whose ardent and unopposed declamation is forceful and lucid, but only apparently logical; a declamation at once disordered, impractical, and potentially sinful insofar as his Utopia (lacking the verisimilitude of God's plan or the efforts of an erected wit) fails to lead us, in Sidney's words, to "know what [rightful] perfectiō is." Hythlodaeus's rhetorical praise of folly is, unlike Erasmus's, then, an *anti*-poetic vision.

The clues we find in the Tudor practices of rhetoric and poetic that tell us where to stand when reading *Utopia* are learned and subtle; the *Utopia* was initially, after all, a private work written for the highly educated band of European humanists, Erasmus foremost among them, to whom Thomas More rushed manuscript copies. We can understand, given his sophisticated art of indirection, why he was both astonished and pleased in the praise accorded *Utopia*, and we can also understand his apprehensions about its reception and his serious misgivings about its publication. They were not—as we learn from some who misunderstood him—groundless. The *Utopia* relies, more heavily than most works, on the implications of the writer and the inferences of the reader.

In this, the *Utopia* remains even today one of the most profoundly humanist works of the Renaissance. Inculcated with belief in the educability of man, exemplary as a work of humanist poetics drawn from humanist rhetoric, the *Utopia* finally depends upon the reader to be interpreter and judge—just as *suasoriae* and *controversiae* and the value of icastic art do. Hythlodaeus is a kind of humanist Everyman whose desires for a better and more reasonable life are betrayed by irrational folly and pride, but his declamations (inherent disputations with us), as they suggest a misguided ontogeny and direct us to a fallen phylogeny in the history of the Utopians, nevertheless suggest urgent human needs and warn us of fundamental human shortcomings: poetry is a propaedeutic to philosophy.

Wayne A. Rebhorn has argued suggestively that the *Utopia* "is based on a particularly unsentimental, Christian view of nature as fallen and in need of human management and labor if it is to be fertile and bear fruit."[57] The idea of cultivation abounds in the *Utopia*—in theme and in image—but the particular lack of any programmatic organization in *Utopia* II, as G. R. Elton has most recently noted,[58] suggests a weakness in Hythlodaeus's presentation and insists once more that, by its cultivating and educating us, we take up Hythlodaeus's slack. The *Utopia*, like the *Moriae encomium*, thus requires that meaning come from the reader, that *we* distinguish reliable rhetoric from sophistry, icastic from irrational art, and so determine what is serious and what is foolish—and where the implied distinction truly lies. The work, as a humanist document, as a play of the mind, instructs (literally, in-structs, or in-forms, builds from within) as it educates (literally, leads us out to resolve its problems). Thomas More's near-contemporary John Colet used the same principle in lecturing at Oxford on Paul's epistles, "Everything is such as the receiver,"[59] because he held the function of the humanist trivium to be that of disciplining the faculties of the reader to cultivate reasoned thought and response. The incomplete declamation of *Utopia* I,

57. "Thomas More's Enclosed Garden: *Utopia* and Renaissance Humanism," *English Literary Renaissance* 6 (1976) 141.

58. In a lecture to the St. Thomas More Society at Yale University, 3 December 1977.

59. *Enarratio in Epistolam S. Pauli ad Romanos*, ed. J. H. Lupton (London 1873) 164, and *Enarratio in Primam Epistolam S. Pauli ad Corinthios*, ed. J. H. Lupton (London 1874) 13, 167; quoted by P. Albert Duhamel, "Medievalism of More's 'Utopia,'" *Studies in Philology* 52 (1955) 101.

like the frustrated disputation of *Utopia* II, requires our own best responses. *Utopia*, John Traugott reminds us, "abandon[s] the reader with the burden of bridging the ironic disjunction between the impossible truth, utopia, which cannot be ignored, and the shadowy actuality, England, which cannot be got rid of."[60] The unchallenged life is not worth living.

60. "A Voyage to Nowhere with Thomas More and Jonathan Swift: *Utopia* and *The Voyage to the Houyhnhnms*," *Sewanee Review* 69 (1961) 536.

Publications of the UCLA Center for Medieval and Renaissance Studies

HUMANA CIVILITAS Series (Undena Publications)

1. *On Pre-Modern Technology and Science: Studies in Honor of Lynn White, jr.* Bert S. Hall and Delno C. West, editors. 1976. 233 pages.
2. *The King's Progress to Jerusalem: Some Interpretations of David during the Reformation Period and Their Patristic and Medieval Background*, by Edward A. Gosselin. 1976. 131 pages.
3. *The Politics of an Erasmian Lawyer, Vasco de Quiroga*, by Ross Dealy. 1976. 33 pages.
4. *Persian Medical Manuscripts at the University of California, Los Angeles: A Descriptive Catalogue*, by Lutz Richter-Bernburg. 1978, xxii + 297 pages.
5. *Rhetoric and Poetic in Thomas More's* Utopia, by Arthur F. Kinney. 1979. 36 pages.

CONTRIBUTIONS Series (University of California Press)

1. *Medieval Secular Literature*. William Matthews, editor. 1965. 89 pages.
2. *Galileo Reappraised*. Carlo L. Golino, editor. 1966. 110 pages.
3. *The Transformation of the Roman World—Gibbon's Problem after Two Centuries*. Lynn White, jr., editor. 1966, 321 pages, hard cover and paperback.
4. *Scientific Methods in Medieval Archaeology*. Rainer Berger, editor. 1970, 459 pages.
5. *Violence and Civil Disorder in Italian Cities, 1200-1500*. Lauro Martines, editor. 1972. 353 pages.
6. *The Darker Vision of the Renaissance*. Robert S. Kinsman, editor. 1974, 352 pages.
7. *The Copernican Achievement*. Robert S. Westman, editor. 1975, 380 pages.
8. *First Images of America: The Impact of the New World on the Old*. Fredi Chiappelli, editor; Michael J. B. Allen and Robert L. Benson, co-editors. 1976, 2 vols., 957 pages.
9. *Friedrich Diez Centennial Lectures* (Supplement to *Romance Philology*, vol. XXX, 2). Edward F. Tuttle, editor. 1976. 30 pages.
10. *Old English Poetry: Essays on Style*. Daniel G. Calder, editor. (in press)

PUBLICATIONS Series (University of California Press)

1. *Dissent and Reform in the Early Middle Ages*, by Jeffrey Burton Russell. 1965, 325 pages.
2. *Leonardo's Legacy: An International Symposium*. C. D. O'Malley, editor. 1969, 255 pages.

3. *Guide to Serial Bibliographies in Medieval Studies*, by Richard H. Rouse, 1969, 150 pages.
4. *The Decline of Medieval Hellenism in Asia Minor and the Process of Islamization from the Eleventh through the Fifteenth Century*, by Speros Vryonis, Jr. 1971, 532 pages.
5. *Christian Political Theory and Church Politics in the Mid-Twelfth Century*, by Stanley Chodorow. 1972, 300 pages.
6. *The Song of Roland: Formulaic Style and Poetic Craft*, by Joseph J. Duggan. 1973. 226 pages.
7. *Studies in Medieval Philosophy, Science, and Logic: Collected Papers, 1933-1969*, by Ernest A. Moody. 1975, 453 pages.
8. *Slavery and Serfdom in the Middle Ages*, selected essays by Marc Bloch. 1975, 276 pages.
9. *Marsilio Ficino: The* Philebus *Commentary, A Critical Edition and Translation*, by Michael J. B. Allen. 1975, 560 pages.
10. *Marius:* On the Elements, *A Critical Edition and Translation*, by Richard C. Dales. 1976, 206 pages.
11. *An Italian Lordship: The Bishopric of Lucca in the Late Middle Ages*, by Duane J. Osheim. 1977, 211 pages.
12. *Pope Alexander III and the Council of Tours (1163)*, by Robert Somerville. 1977, 110 pages.
13. *Medieval Religion and Technology: Collected Essays*, by Lynn White, jr. 1978. 360 pages.

INDEPENDENT Publications

1. *Leonardo da Vinci: Studies for a Nativity and the "Mona Lisa Cartoon" with drawings after Leonardo from the Elmer Belt Library of Vinciana*, by Carlo Pedretti. 1973, 49 pages.
2. *In Honor of the Eightieth Birthday of Dr. Elmer Belt, Physician, Scholar and One Who Loves Nature*, by William A. Emboden, Jr. 1973, 20 pages, out of print.
3. *Boccaccio: Secoli di vita* (Proceedings of the International Symposium on Boccaccio, 1975). Marga Cottino-Jones and Edward F. Tuttle, editors. 1977. 310 pages (Angelo Longo Editore).
4. *Medieval and Renaissance Manuscripts at the University of California, Los Angeles: Preliminary Descriptions*, by Mirella Ferrari. 1978, 376 pages.
5. *The Dawn of Modern Banking* (Proceedings of a conference at UCLA, September 1977). 1979. 321 pages (Yale University Press).

JOURNALS

Viator: Medieval and Renaissance Studies (annually since 1970; University of California Press) is a hard-cover journal which averages 350-450 pages; its primary, but not exclusive, focus is intercultural and interdisciplinary research. *Viator* does not include reviews or current news.

Comitatus (annually since 1970, sponsored by the Center since 1973; Undena Publications) contains articles in the field of Medieval and Renaissance studies by University of California graduate students.